"At Christmas play and make good cheer,
for Christmas comes but once a year."

Thomas Tusser, 16th Century

Children's
Christmas
Songbook

Amsco Publications
London / New York / Paris / Sydney / Copenhagen / Madrid / Tokyo / Berlin

Exclusive distributors:

Music Sales Limited
8/9 Frith Street, London W1D 3JB, England.

Music Sales Corporation
257 Park Avenue South, New York, NY10010,
United States of America.

Music Sales Pty Limited
120 Rothschild Avenue, Rosebery,
NSW 2018, Australia.

Order No. AM982498
ISBN 1-84449-990-1
This book © Copyright 2005 by
Amsco Publications.

Compiled by Alison Hedger & Heather Ramage.
Recipes, games and crafts selected and/or
written by Alison Hedger.
Edited by Heather Ramage.
Music processed by Jerry Lanning & Enigma.
Designed & art directed by Michael Bell Design.
Illustrated by Lesley Saddington.
Printed in Peru by Quebecor World.

Your Guarantee of Quality:
As publishers, we strive to produce every
book to the highest commercial standards.
The music has been carefully designed to
minimize awkward page turns and to make
playing from it a real pleasure.
Particular care has been given to specifying
acid-free, neutral-sized paper made from pulps
which have not been elemental chlorine bleached.
This pulp is from farmed sustainable
forests and was produced with special regard
for the environment.
Throughout, the printing and binding have been
planned to ensure a sturdy, attractive publication
which should give years of enjoyment.
If your copy fails to meet our high standards,
please inform us and we will gladly replace it.

www.musicsales.com

Poems...

Action *Rhymes...*

Stories...

Crafts...

Recipes...

Games...

Music...

Angels *From* The *Realms* Of Glory

Words by **James Montgomery** *Music* **Traditional French**

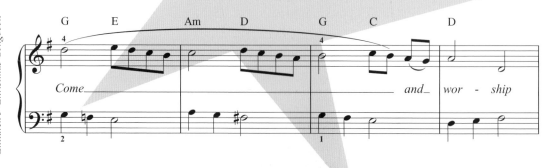

Christ, the new - born King,___ come_____

_____ and_ wor - ship, wor - ship Christ, the new - born King.

2
Shepherds, in the field abiding,
Watching o'er your flocks by night,
God with us is now residing,
Yonder shines the infant light:
Come and worship…

3
Sages, leave your contemplations;
Brighter visions beam afar:
Seek the great Desire of Nations;
Ye have seen his natal star:
Come and worship…

4
Saints before the alter bending,
Watching long in hope and fear,
Suddenly the Lord, descending,
In His temple shall appear:
Come and worship…

5
Though an infant now we view Him,
He shall fill his Father's throne,
Gather all the nations to him;
Ev'ry knee shall then bow down:
Come and worship…

Away *In A Manger*

Words & Music by **William James Kirkpatrick**

1. A-way in a man-ger, no crib for a

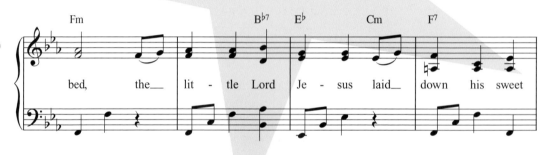

bed, the lit-tle Lord Je-sus laid down his sweet

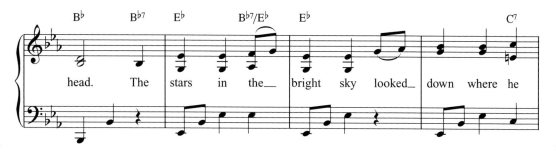

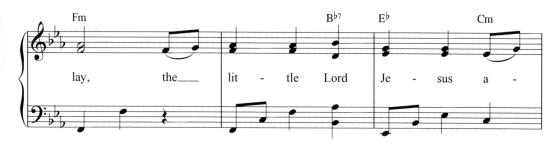

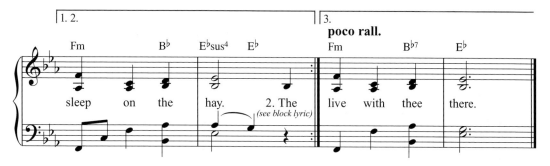

The cattle are lowing, the baby awakes,
2 But little Lord Jesus no crying he makes.
I love thee, Lord Jesus! Look down from the sky,
And stay by my side until morning is nigh.

Be near me, Lord Jesus; I ask thee to stay
3 Close by me for ever, and love me, I pray.
Bless all the dear children in thy tender care,
And fit us for heaven, to live with thee there.

Away In A Manger

US Tune Words by **William James Kirkpatrick** *Music by* **James R Murray**

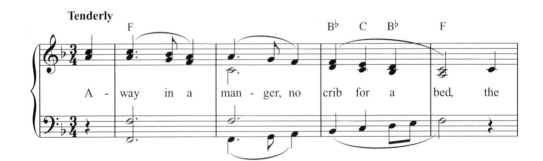

A - way   in a   man - ger, no   crib   for   a   bed,   the

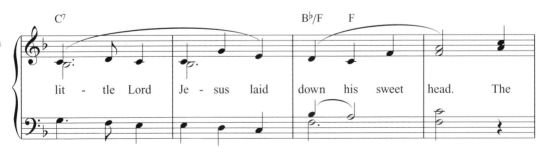

lit — tle Lord Je - sus laid down his sweet head. The

Children's Christmas Songbook

stars   in   the   sky____ looked   down   where   he   lay,   the

lit - tle   Lord   Je - sus   a - sleep   in   the   hay.

2 The cattle are lowing, the baby awakes,
But little Lord Jesus no crying he makes.
I love thee, Lord Jesus! Look down from the sky,
And stay by my side until morning is nigh.

3 Be near me, Lord Jesus; I ask thee to stay
Close by me for ever, and love me, I pray.
Bless all the dear children in thy tender care,
And fit us for heaven, to live with thee there.

A Star
Traditional

Star light, star bright,
First star I see tonight,
I wish I may, I wish I might
Have the wish I wish tonight.

Coventry Carol

Traditional

Moderately

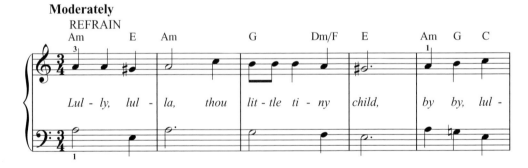

Lul - ly, lul - la, thou lit - tle ti - ny child, by by, lul-

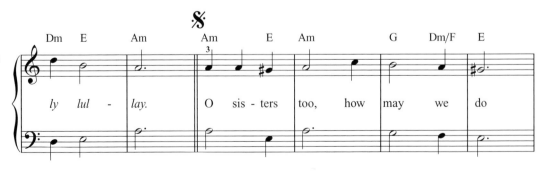

ly lul - lay. O sis - ters too, how may we do

Children's Christmas Songbook

11

for to pre - serve this day? This poor young - ling for

D.S. then refrain
after verse 3

whom we do sing, by by, lul - ly lul - lay.

2
Herod, the king, in his raging,
Chargèd he hath this day,
His men of might, in his own sight,
All young children to slay.

3
That woe is me, poor child for thee!
And ever morn and day,
For thy parting neither say nor sing
By by, lully lullay!

REFRAIN
Lully, lulla, thou little tiny child,
By by, lully lullay.

Deck *The* Hall

Traditional Welsh

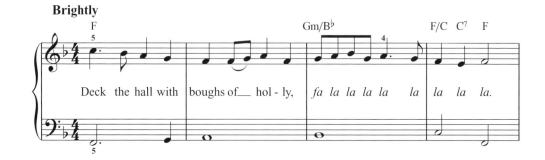

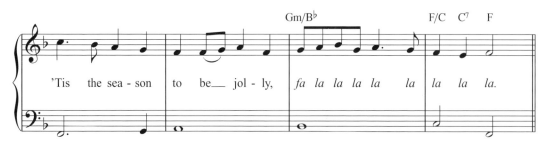

Brightly

Deck the hall with boughs of__ hol - ly, *fa la la la la   la   la   la   la.*

'Tis   the sea - son   to be__ jol - ly, *fa la la la la   la   la   la   la.*

Children's Christmas Songbook

Fill the mead cup, drain the bar-rel, *fa la la   la la la   la la la.*

Troll the an-cient Christ-mas_ car-ol, *fa la la la la   la   la la la.*

2
See the flowing bowl before us,
Fa la la la la la la la la,
Strike the harp and join the chorus,
Fa la la la la la la la la,
Follow me in merry measure,
Fa la la la la la la la la,
While I sing of beauty's treasure,
Fa la la la la la la la la.

3
Fast away the old year passes,
Fa la la la la la la la la,
Hail the new, ye lads and lassies,
Fa la la la la la la la la,
Laughing, quaffing, all together,
Fa la la la la la la la la,
Heedless of the wind and weather.
Fa la la la la la la la la.

Ding *Dong!* Merrily *On* High

Words by **George Ratcliffe Woodward** *Music* **Traditional French**

Ding dong! Mer - ri - ly on high, in heav'n the bells are ring - ing.

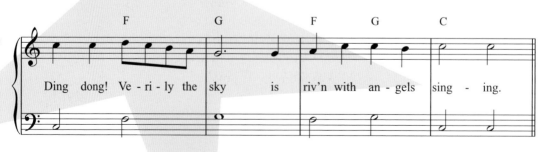

Ding dong! Ve - ri - ly the sky is riv'n with an - gels sing - ing.

Children's Christmas Songbook

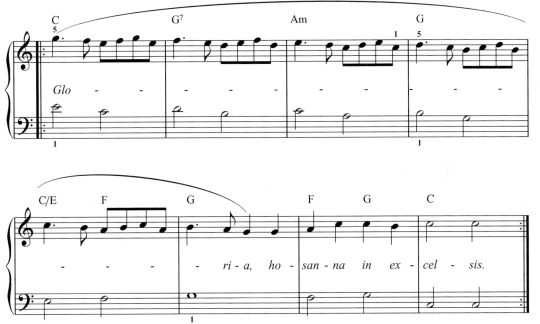

Glo - - - - - - - - - - - ri - a, ho - san - na in ex - cel - sis.

2 E'en so here below, below,
Let steeple bells be swungen,
And i-o, i-o, i-o,
By priest and people sungen.
Gloria, hosanna in excelsis…

3 Pray you, dutifully prime
Your matin chime, ye ringers;
May you beautifully rhyme
Your evetime song, ye singers.
Gloria, hosanna in excelsis…

God *Rest* You *Merry*, Gentlemen

Traditional

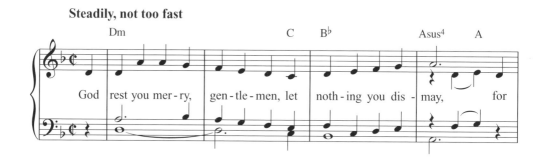

Steadily, not too fast

God rest you mer-ry, gen-tle-men, let noth-ing you dis-may, for Je-sus Christ our Sa-viour was born on Christ-mas Day, to

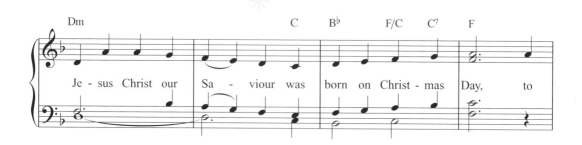

save us all from Sa-tan's pow'r when we were gone a-stray

Children's Christmas Songbook

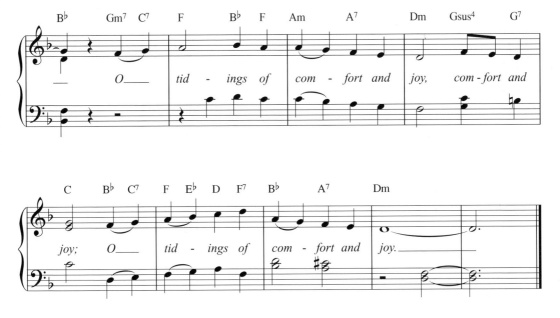

2 In Bethlehem, in Jewry,
   This blessèd babe was born,
   And laid within a manger,
   Upon this blessèd morn;
   The which his mother Mary
   Did nothing take in scorn.
   O tidings of comfort and joy…

3 From God, our heav'nly Father,
   A blessèd angel came,
   And unto certain shepherds
   Brought tidings of the same
   How that in Bethlehem was born
   The Son of God by name.
   O tidings of comfort and joy…

4 'Fear not,' then said the angel,
   'Let nothing you affright,
   This day is born a Saviour,
   Of virtue, pow'r and might;
   By Him the world is overcome
   And Satan put to flight.'
   O tidings of comfort and joy…

5 The shepherds at those tidings
   Rejoicèd much in mind,
   And left their flocks a-feeding,
   In tempest, storm and wind,
   And went to Bethlehem straightway
   This blessèd babe to find.
   O tidings of comfort and joy…

6 But when to Bethlehem they came,
   Whereat this infant lay,
   They found him in a manger,
   Where oxen feed on hay;
   His mother Mary kneeling,
   Unto the Lord did pray.
   O tidings of comfort and joy…

7 Now to the Lord sing praises,
   All you within this place,
   And with true love and fellowship
   Each other now embrace;
   This holy tide of Christmas
   All others doth deface.
   O tidings of comfort and joy…

Good *King* Wenceslas

Words by **J M Neale** *Music* **Traditional**

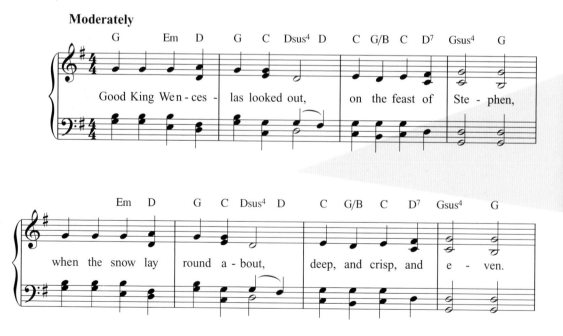

Children's Christmas Songbook

Brightly shone the moon that night, though the frost was cruel,
when a poor man came in sight, gath-'ring winter fuel.

2 'Hither, page, and stand by me,
If thou know'st it, telling,
Yonder peasant, who is he,
Where and what his dwelling?'
'Sire, he lives a good league hence,
Underneath the mountain,
Right against the forest fence,
By Saint Agnes' fountain.'

3 'Bring me flesh, and bring me wine,
Bring me pine-logs hither:
Thou and I will see him dine,
When we bring them thither.'
Page and monarch, forth they went,
Forth they went together;
Through the rude wind's wild lament,
And the bitter weather.

4 'Sire, the night is darker now,
And the wind blows stronger;
Fails my heart, I know not how;
I can go no longer.'
'Mark my footsteps good, my page;
Tread thou in them boldly:
Thou shalt find the winter's rage
Freeze thy blood less coldly.'

5 In his master's steps he trod,
Where the snow lay dinted;
Heat was in the very sod
Which the Saint had printed.
Therefore, Christians all, be sure,
Wealth or rank possessing,
Ye who now will bless the poor,
Shall yourselves find blessing.

O Holy Night

By **A Adam**

With movement

O ho-ly night,___ the stars are bright-ly shin - ing, it is the

night of the dear Sav-iour's birth!___ Long lay the

Children's Christmas Songbook

O Holy Night

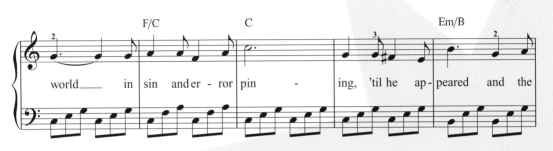

world____ in sin and er - ror pin - ing, 'til he ap - peared and the

soul felt his worth._____ A thrill of hope the

wea - ry soul re - joi - ces, for yon - der breaks the new and glo - rious

morn! Fall_____ on your knees,_____ o

The *Fir*-Tree
by *Hans* Christian *Andersen*

Once upon a time there was a little Fir-tree that lived in the woods. The place he had was a good one; the sun shone on him, he had plenty of fresh air and around him grew many large-sized pines and other firs, but the little Fir wanted so very much to be a grown-up tree just like his neighbours. Children often came along and would say "Oh how pretty he is! What a nice little fir," but this was what the tree could not bear to hear.

At the end of that year, the little Fir had shot up a good deal, and after another year he was taller still, but the other trees continued to tower above him making him feel ever-so small.

"Oh, if only I could be as tall as the other trees," he cried. "Then I would be able to spread out my branches and look over the whole wide world! Birds would build nests amongst my branches and when there was a breeze, I could bend with as much stateliness as the others!"

Neither the sunbeams, nor the birds, nor the red clouds in the morning and evening that sailed above him gave the little Fir any pleasure.

In winter, when the snow lay glistening on the ground, a hare would often come leaping along and jump right over the little Fir.

"Grrrrr!" he fumed. "It makes me so angry that a creature as small as a hare can still bounce over me with little effort," but three winters later and the tree had grown so much that now the hare was obliged to go around him.

"To grow and grow, to get older and be tall," thought the Fir, "is the most delightful thing in the world!"

In autumn, the woodcutters always came and felled some of the largest trees. This happened every year and the young Fir-tree, who had now grown to an ample size, trembled at the sight! The big trees fell to earth with a crash and their branches were chopped off making them look long and bare. They were then laid on carts and dragged by horses out of the woods.

"Where did they go?" thought the Fir. "What became of them?

In spring, the Fir asked the Swallows and the Storks where the big trees went every autumn. The Swallows knew nothing but the Stork nodded his head and said,

"Yes, I think I know. On returning from my travels abroad, I see ships sailing on the sea and often take a rest on their tall, magnificent masts. I am certain that these masts smell most strongly of fir! May I congratulate you, for they lifted themselves on high most majestically!"

"Oh, if only I were old enough to fly across the sea!" said the Fir wistfully. "Oh please Mr. Stork, tell me what it's like?"

"It would take too long to explain," he said curtly. And with that, off he went.

Over the next few months the rain, sun and wind all helped the Fir-tree grow more and more. When Christmas came around, a few young trees were cut down, their branches still intact, and taken away.

"Where are they going to?" asked the Fir. "They are not much taller than I; in fact there was one that was considerably shorter – and why do they retain all their branches?"

We know, we know!" chirped the Sparrows. "We have peeped through the windows in the town! The greatest grandeur awaits them – we saw them in a warm room covered in many splendid ornaments, gingerbread and lights!"

"And then," asked the Fir-tree, "what happens then?"

"We did not see anything more," they chirped back. "It was very beautiful though!"

"Oh, if only I could be a decorated tree! If only I were already on the cart! What a glorious career – it is even better than crossing the sea," the Fir-tree sighed.

"Were I in a warm room with all the splendour and magnificence, then something better, something still grander will surely follow – but what?" he mused. "Oh, how I suffer!"

Throughout the next year, the sun, rain and wind helped the Fir-tree to grow even more and finally, towards the following Christmas, he was one of the first cut down. He felt sad that he would have to leave his home and all his friends the little bushes, flowers and birds, but wondered what excitement lay ahead.

The next thing the Fir heard was a man say, "That one is splendid; we don't want the others."

Then two servants carried him into a large drawing room. Portraits hung on the walls, a grand wood-fire roared and near the white porcelain stove stood two large Chinese vases. There were comfy chairs, silken sofas and large tables full of picture books and toys.

The Fir-tree was placed upright in a pot filled with sand on some brightly coloured carpet. How he quivered! What was to happen to him?

Moments later, servants and young ladies decorated him with sweetie horns, apples, walnuts, and blue and white tapers were placed amongst the leaves. Finally, a large gold tinsel star was placed on top.

"How beautiful it looks!" they all exclaimed. "How it will shine this evening."

"Oh," thought the Fir, "if only this evening would come quickly! I wonder what will happen when the tapers are lighted! Perhaps the other trees in the forest will come and look at me. Perhaps the Sparrows will beat against the window pane. I wonder if a will take root here and stand here all the year round!" He began to get so impatient with the whole matter that he developed a pain in his trunk (which is the same thing as a headache for us).

The tapers were now lighted. What brightness and splendour! The Fir-tree trembled so much that a taper set fire to one of his branches!

"Help, help!" shouted one of the ladies, and quickly put out the fire.

Then suddenly, a group of children and elders entered and they all stood by the tree quite still, looking in awe. Soon enough though, they were all rejoicing and dancing around the Fir-tree, pulling one present after another from underneath.

"What's going on?" wondered the Fir-tree. "What will happen now?"

The lights burned down to the very branches and were put out. Then the children were given permission from their elders to plunder the Tree. So they jumped upon it with such violence that all its branches cracked. If it had not been firmly placed in its pot, it would have certainly tumbled down! The children danced and played. No-one looked at the tree – they were too busy having fun.

"A story, a story!" cried the children, and for the rest of the evening a handsome man told of Klumpy-Dumpy, who fell down the stairs, became King and then married a Princess!

"Maybe that is what the future holds for me," wondered the Fir-tree.

"Who knows, perhaps I may fall down the stairs and get a princess as my wife!" With that thought, the Tree went to sleep dreaming of what joys tomorrow would bring.

In the morning, the maid came in.

"Now, the splendour will begin again!" thought the Fir-tree excitedly, but instead she dragged him out of the room and up the stairs into a loft where no daylight could enter.

"What is the meaning of this?" thought the Tree. "What am I to do here?" He leaned up against a wall and pondered on his predicament. Time enough he had too for his reflections, as days and nights passed and nobody came up to see him. He had been entirely forgotten.

"Of course!" he thought suddenly. "It is now winter and with the cold weather, the ground is far too hard to plant me back, so they are keeping me here until the spring when it gets warmer. How thoughtful of them! If only it weren't so lonely."

"Squeak, squeak!" said a little mouse and popped out of his hole. Then came another, and another. They snuggled around the Fir-tree's branches and one of them said, "This place would be delightful if it wasn't so cold. Isn't that right old Fir?"

"I am by no means old," corrected the Fir. "There are many a Fir older than I!"

"Where do you come from?" enquired the mice. "Tell us all about what you do and about all your adventures!"

"Well," said the Fir, "I come from a little wood where the sun shines and the birds sing..." and he went on to tell the little mice all about his life in the wood.

"Wow! You must have been really happy there old Fir," they said when he had finished.

"I am by no means old," he corrected again. "Yes, now I think about it, they were very happy times." He sighed, realising that maybe he should have appreciated what he had rather than always wishing for something better.

"What delightful stories you know," said the mice. "Tell us another!" And so the Fir told them about Klumpy-Dumpy and how he dreamed of marrying a princess himself one day.

The next night, more mice came and so did a few rats, but the rats were not impressed with the Fir-tree's stories.

Children's Christmas Songbook

"Don't you know any stories about bacon or cheese, or other tasty food?" they said, and eventually both the mice and rats got fed up with the Fir-tree's tales and went away, never to come back. Fir-tree was on his own again.

Finally, there was movement in the loft. Some people started to clear things away and the Fir-tree was pulled out and dropped roughly onto the landing below.

"Now a merry life will begin again!" he shouted with glee, as he was taken outside into the sunshine. He stretched out his branches but to his horror, they were all withered and yellow, and instead of being planted back in the ground, he was thrown into a corner amongst some weeds and nettles. The golden star left over from Christmas Day was still on the top, glistening in the sunshine.

"Look at that ugly old Fir-tree," mocked some children who were playing nearby. They approached, but only to whip the golden star from the top and run off.

"If only I were back in the loft with the little mice," he cried. "If only I were back in the warm room with all the joyful dancing and stories; if only I were back in the wood with all my friends the flowers and the birds. It's all over! It's past! How I should have been grateful when I had reason to be!"

And with that, the woodcutter chopped the Fir-tree into small pieces and left them in a heap ready to be lit later that day. The children played about in the court and the youngest wore the golden star on his breast, the star the Tree had worn on one of the happiest evenings of his life.

However, that was over now, the Fir-tree gone and the story at an end. After all, every tale must end at last.

Summarised version by Heather Ramage.

Long, Long Ago
Anon

Winds through the olive trees softly did blow
Round little Bethlehem, long, long ago.
Sheep on the hillside lay white as the snow;
Shepherds were watching them, long, long ago.

Then from the happy skies angels bent low,
Singing their songs of joy, long, long ago.
For, in his manger bed, cradled we know,
Christ came to Bethlehem, long, long ago.

Hark! *The* Herald *Angels* Sing

Words by **Charles Wesley**   *Music by* **Felix Mendelssohn**

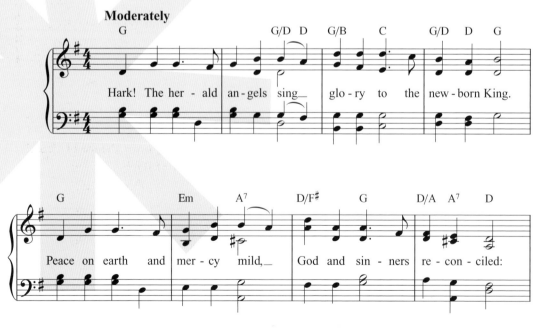

Children's Christmas Songbook

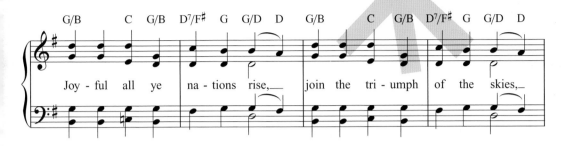

Joy - ful all ye | na - tions rise,__ | join the tri - umph | of the skies,__

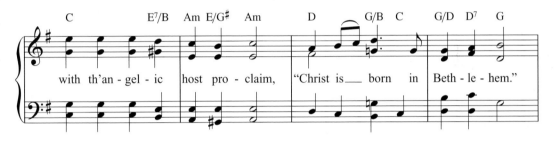

with th'an - gel - ic | host pro - claim, | "Christ is__ born in | Beth - le - hem."

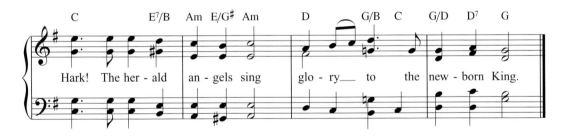

Hark! The her - ald | an - gels sing | glo - ry__ to the | new - born King.

2
Christ, by highest heav'n adored,
Christ, the everlasting Lord,
Late in time behold him come,
Offspring of a Virgin's womb!
Veiled in flesh the Godhead see,
Hail, the incarnate Deity!
Pleased as man with us to dwell,
Jesus, our Emmanuel.
Hark! The herald angels sing etc…

3
Hail, the heav'n-born Prince of Peace!
Hail, the Sun of Righteousness!
Light and life to all he brings,
Ris'n with healing in his wings;
Mild he lays His glory by,
Born that we no more may die,
Born to raise us from the earth,
Born to give us second birth.
Hark! The herald angels sing etc…

In *Dulci* Jubilo

English Words by **R L Pearsall** *Music* **Traditional**

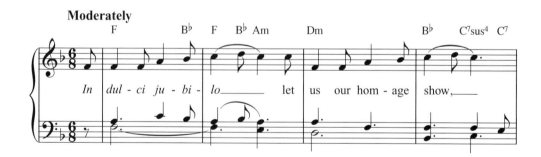

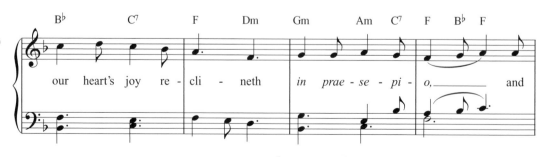

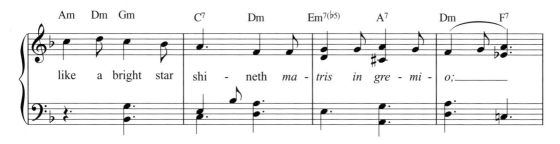

like   a   bright   star   shi - neth   ma - tris   in   gre - mi - o;_____

al - pha   es   et   o,_____   al - pha   es   et   o!_____

2

O Jesu parvule!
My heart is sore for thee!
Hear me, I beseech thee,
O puer optime!
My prayer let it reach thee
O Princeps gloriae!
Trahe me post te!
Trahe me post te!

3

O Patris caritas!
O nati lenitas!
Deep were we stainèd
Per nostra crimina;
But thou has for us gainèd
Coelorum gaudia:
O that we were there,
O that we were there!

4

Ubi sunt gaudia, where,
If that they be not there?
There, are angels singing
Nova cantica;
There the bells are ringing
In Regis curia:
O that we were there,
O that we were there!

I *Saw* Three *Ships*

Traditional

With a lilt

I saw three ships come sail-ing in, on Christ-mas day, on Christ-mas day, I

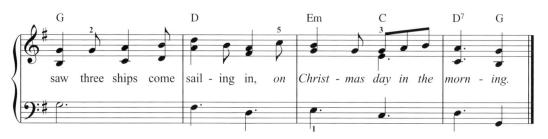

saw three ships come sail-ing in, on Christ-mas day in the morn-ing.

2 And what was in those ships all three?
On Christmas Day, on Christmas Day,
And what was in those ships all three?
On Christmas Day in the morning.

3 Our Saviour Christ and his lady.
On Christmas Day, on Christmas Day,
Our Saviour Christ and his lady.
On Christmas Day in the morning.

4 Pray, whither sailed those ships all three?
On Christmas Day, on Christmas Day,
Pray, whither sailed those ships all three?
On Christmas Day in the morning.

5 O, they sailed into Bethlehem.
On Christmas Day, on Christmas Day,
O, they sailed into Bethlehem.
On Christmas Day in the morning.

6 And all the bells on earth shall ring.
On Christmas Day, on Christmas Day,
And all the bells on earth shall ring.
On Christmas Day in the morning.

7 And all the angels in heaven shall sing.
On Christmas Day, on Christmas Day,
And all the angels in heaven shall sing.
On Christmas Day in the morning.

8 And all the souls on earth shall sing.
On Christmas Day, on Christmas Day,
And all the souls on earth shall sing.
On Christmas Day in the morning.

9 Then let us all rejoice amain!
On Christmas Day, on Christmas Day,
Then let us all rejoice amain!
On Christmas Day in the morning.

It *Came* Upon *The* Midnight *Clear*

Words by **Edmund Hamilton Sears** *Music* **Traditional**

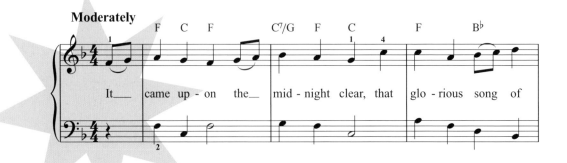

It__ came up - on the__ mid - night clear, that glo - rious song of

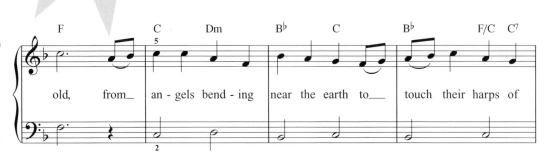

old, from__ an - gels bend - ing near the earth to__ touch their harps of

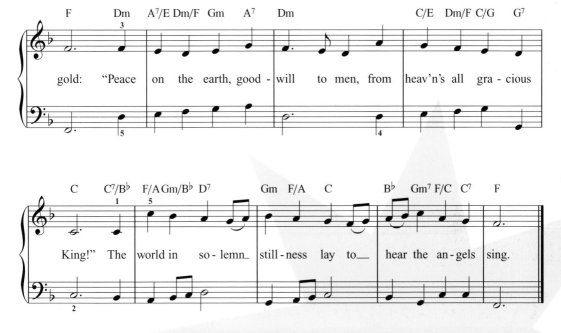

gold: "Peace on the earth, good-will to men, from heav'n's all gra-cious

King!" The world in so-lemn_ still-ness lay to_ hear the an-gels sing.

2 Still through the cloven skies they come,
With peaceful wings unfurled;
And still their heav'nly music floats
O'er all the weary world:
Above its sad and lowly plains
They bend on hov'ring wing;
And ever o'er its Babel-sounds
The blessèd angels sing.

3 Yet with the woes of sin and strife
The world has suffered long;
Beneath the angel-strain have rolled
Two-thousand years of wrong;
And warring humandkind hears not
The love-song which they bring:
O hush the noise of mortal strife,
And hear the angels sing!

4 And ye, beneath life's crushing load,
Whose forms are bending low,
Who toil along the climbing way
With painful steps and slow:
Look now! For glad and golden hours
Come swiftly on the wing;
O rest beside the weary road,
And hear the angels sing.

5 For lo, the days are hast'ning on,
By prophets seen of old,
When with the ever-circling years
Comes round the age of gold;
When peace shall over all the earth
Its ancient splendours fling,
And all the world give back the song
Which now the angels sing.

It *Came* Upon *The* Midnight *Clear*

US Tune Words by **Edmund Hamilton Sears** *Music by* ***Richard Storrs Willis***

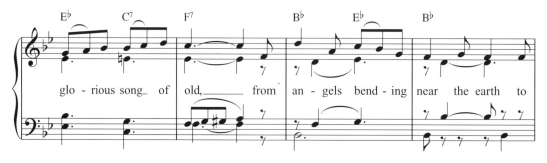

1. It came up-on the mid-night clear, that

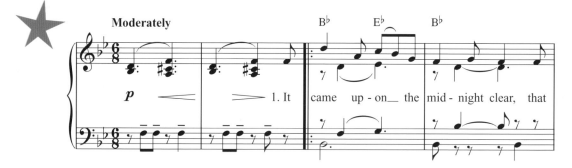

glo-rious song of old, from an-gels bend-ing near the earth to

touch their harps of gold: "Peace on the earth, good-will to men from

Children's Christmas Songbook

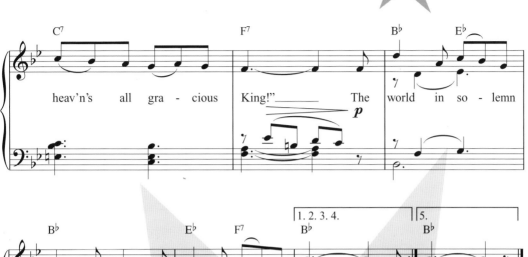

heav'n's   all   gra - cious   King!"_____   The   world   in   so - lemn

still - ness   lay   to   hear   the   an - gels   sing._____   2.Still   sing._____

(see block lyric)

2
Still through the cloven skies they come,
With peaceful wings unfurled;
And still their heav'nly music floats
O'er all the weary world:
Above its sad and lowly plains
They bend on hov'ring wing;
And ever o'er its Babel-sounds
The blessèd angels sing.

3
Yet with the woes of sin and strife
The world has suffered long;
Beneath the angel-strain have rolled
Two-thousand years of wrong;
And warring humandkind hears not
The love-song which they bring:
O hush the noise of mortal strife,
And hear the angels sing!

4
And ye, beneath life's crushing load,
Whose forms are bending low,
Who toil along the climbing way
With painful steps and slow:
Look now! For glad and golden hours
Come swiftly on the wing;
O rest beside the weary road,
And hear the angels sing.

5
For lo, the days are hast'ning on,
By prophets seen of old,
When with the ever-circling years
Comes round the age of gold;
When peace shall over all the earth
Its ancient splendours fling,
And all the world give back the song
Which now the angels sing.

Joy *To* The *World*

Words by **Isaac Watts**   *Music by* **George Frideric Handel**

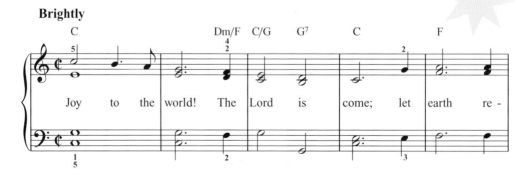

Joy to the world! The Lord is come; let earth re-

38

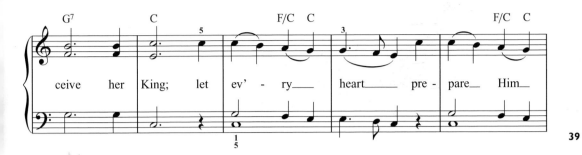

ceive   her | King;   let | ev' - ry___ | heart___   pre - | pare__   Him__

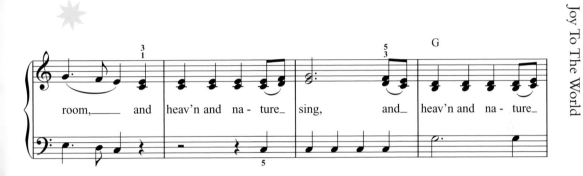

room,___   and | heav'n and na - ture_ | sing,   and_ | heav'n and na - ture_

sing,   and_ | hea - ven,   and | hea -   ven and | na - ture | sing.

2 Joy to the earth! The Saviour reigns;
Let us our songs employ;
While fields and floods, rocks, hills and plains
Repeat the sounding joy,
Repeat the sounding joy,
Repeat, repeat the sounding joy.

3 He rules the world with truth and grace,
And makes the nations prove
The glories of his righteousness,
And wonders of his love,
And wonders of his love,
And wonders, and wonders of his love.

O Christmas *Tree* (O Tannenbaum)

Traditional

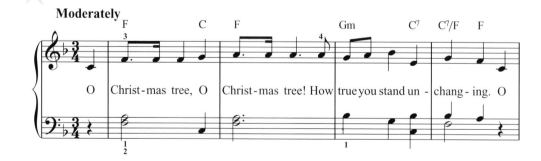

Moderately

O | Christ-mas tree, O | Christ-mas tree! How | true you stand un - | chang - ing. O

Children's Christmas Songbook

Christ - mas tree, O Christ - mas tree! How true you stand un - chang - ing. Your

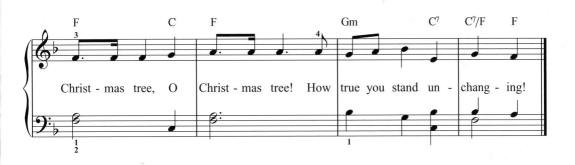

boughs so green in sum - mer - time, re - main so green in win - ter - time. O

Christ - mas tree, O Christ - mas tree! How true you stand un - chang - ing!

2

O Christmas Tree, O Christmas Tree!
Thou hast a wonderous message.
O Christmas Tree, O Christmas Tree!
Thou hast a wonderous message.
Thou dost proclaim the Saviour's birth,
Goodwill to men and peace on earth.
O Christmas Tree, O Christmas Tree!
Thou hast a wonderous message.

O Come *All* Ye *Faithful*

Original Words & Music by **John Francis Wade**

English Words by **Frederick Oakeley**

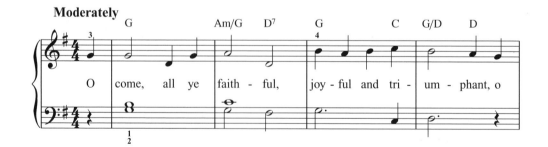

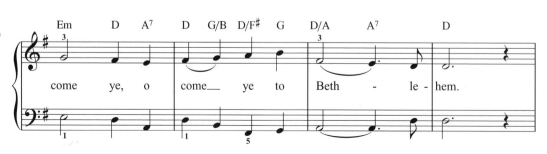

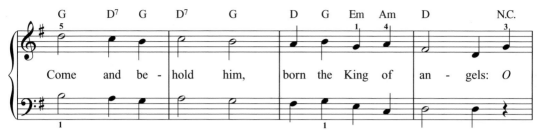

Come and be - hold him, born the King of an - gels: O

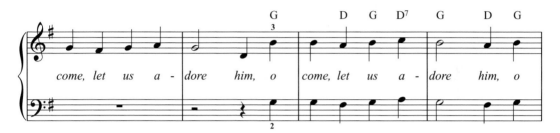

come, let us a - dore him, o come, let us a - dore him, o

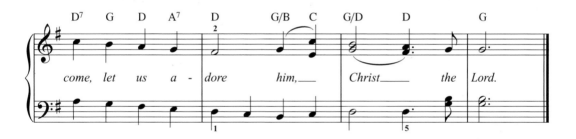

come, let us a - dore him,___ Christ____ the Lord.

2 God of God,
Light of light,
Lo! He abhors not the Virgin's womb;
Very God, begotten, not created:
O come, let us adore him…

3 Sing choirs of angels,
Sing in exultation,
Sing all ye citizens of heav'n above;
Glory to God in the highest:
O come, let us adore him…

4 Yea, Lord, we greet thee,
Born this happy morning,
Jesu, to thee be glory giv'n;
Word of the Father, now in flesh appearing:
O come, let us adore him…

O Come, *O Come*, Emmanuel

Traditional English Words by **John Neale**

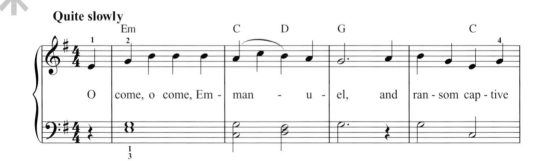

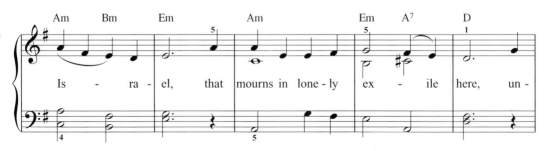

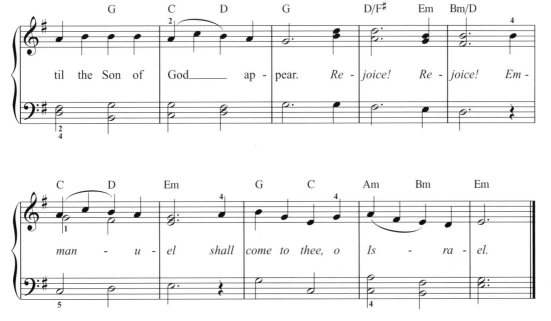

G   C   D   G   D/F♯   Em   Bm/D

til the Son of God_____ ap - pear. Re - joice! Re - joice! Em -

C   D   Em   G   C   Am   Bm   Em

man - u - el shall come to thee, o Is - ra - el.

2
O come, thou rod of Jesse, free
Thine own from Satan's tyranny;
From depths of hell thy people save,
And give them vict'ry o'er the grave.
Rejoice! Rejoice!...

3
O come, thou dayspring, come and cheer
Our spirits by thine advent here;
Disperse the gloomy clouds of night,
And death's dark shadows put to flight.
Rejoice! Rejoice!...

4
O come, thou key of David, come,
And open wide our heav'nly home;
Make safe the way that leads on high,
And close the path to misery.
Rejoice! Rejoice!...

5
O come, o come, thou Lord of might,
Who to thy tribes, on Sinai's height
In ancient times didst give the Law
In cloud, and majesty and awe.
Rejoice! Rejoice!...

The *First* Nowell

Traditional

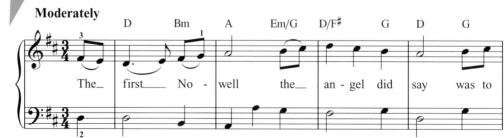

The_ first___ No - well the_ an - gel did say was to

Children's Christmas Songbook

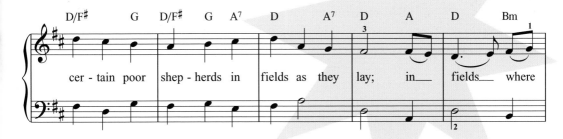

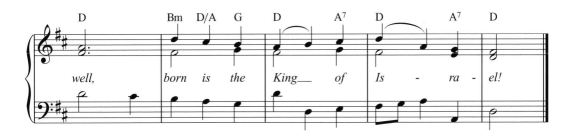

2 They lookèd up and saw a star,
Shining in the east, beyond them far,
And to the earth it gave great light,
And so it continued both day and night.
Nowell, Nowell…

3 And by the light of that same star,
Three wise men came from country far;
To seek for a king was their intent,
And to follow the star wherever it went.
Nowell, Nowell…

4 This star drew nigh to the north-west,
O'er Bethlehem it took its rest,
And there it did both stop and stay
Right over the place where Jesus lay.
Nowell, Nowell…

5 Then entered in those wise men three,
Full rev'rently upon their knee,
And offered there in his presence,
Their gold and myrrh and frankincense.
Nowell, Nowell…

6 Then let us all with one accord
Sing praises to our heav'nly Lord,
That hath made heav'n and earth of naught,
And with his blood mankind hath bought.
Nowell, Nowell…

Little Jack Horner

Anon

Little Jack Horner
Sat in the corner
Eating his Christmas pie.
He put in his thumb
And pulled out a plum
And said, "What a good boy am I."

Jan *And* The *Christmas* Tree

Traditional Czechoslovakian story retold by Alison Hedger

Jan cleared the snow from the sill and pressed his cold nose up to the window pane. He gasped at the magnificent banqueting hall and the sumptuous Christmas feast. The long tables were laden with food and beautifully dressed women and handsome men were eating, drinking, talking and laughing. The air was buzzing with happiness and everything seemed to glow. At the far end of the hall Jan could see a gorgeously decorated tall Christmas tree. A silver doll angel with wings of beaten gold sat sparkling high up on the top of the tree.

"I'll be alright here," thought Jan. "These fine people will be sure to give a poor, homeless, hungry orphan like me something nice to eat." So he called out three times in his loudest voice: "Hello, I'm Jan the orphan who seeks food and shelter this Christmas Eve," but no one took any notice; everyone just carried on talking and feasting.

"How silly I am!" Jan exclaimed. "Rich people have no time for me – I should have realised. Never mind, I'll go and find a merchant's house and see if I can find food and shelter there."

So Jan set off through the new soft snow and came to a street with tall, smart houses.

"This looks like the right place," Jan said to himself.

He looked through a window and saw candles burning and a well-dressed lady concentrating hard on painting gold onto gingerbread figures. There was a fine Christmas tree in the middle of the room, and the merchant was decorating the branches with wooden storks with silver beaks and stags with golden antlers.

"These people look very comfortable and kind," thought Jan, and he called out three times:

"Hello, I'm Jan the orphan who seeks food and shelter this Christmas Eve," but neither the man nor the woman took any notice – they were too wrapped up in their own thoughts to hear Jan's voice.

"How silly I am!" Jan exclaimed. "Busy people have no time for me – I should have realised. Never mind, perhaps I'll go and find a peasant's house and see if I can find food and shelter there."

So Jan set off through the deep snow and came to the poorest part of the town. He peered through the little window and saw the dancing light of a log fire. The wife was busy cooking and her children sang as they held hands and danced around a small Christmas tree.

"How happy they look!" thought Jan, and he called out three times:

"Hello, I'm Jan the orphan who seeks food and shelter this Christmas Eve," but the laughter and singing was too loud for Jan to be heard and no one took any notice of him.

"Even the peasants have no room for an orphan on Christmas Eve," sighed Jan as big tears rolled down his cheeks. He turned away and sadly walked towards the town square. He saw a child of his own age coming towards him, holding a lighted lantern.

"Why are you crying?" asked the child.

"Because everyone in Prague has family, a home, food and a Christmas tree. Everyone that is, except me!" cried Jan. "I knocked three times and called out, but no one hears me."

Just then, Jan noticed through his warm tears, that the child was shivering in the cold and snowflakes were settling on his hair. This child had no coat!

"But you are less fortunate than I am," said Jan. "At least I have a thick coat to keep me warm."

He took off his old brown coat and gave it to the child who put it on. An old woman shuffled by, huddled up in a blanket.

"What on earth are two children doing out here in the cold on Christmas Eve?" she asked.

"I've no home to go to," answered Jan "and there's no one who'll give me food and shelter."

"Indeed there is!" said the old woman. "I'll take you in and you can share all that I have – follow me, it's not far."

She turned into the next alleyway and went down into a cellar where several ragged but happy children greeted her.

"This is my family – all orphan children like yourself," she said proudly. "Come in."

She threw a small log onto the little fire on which a big pot of hot soup was warming. The old woman ladled the soup into wooden bowls. Everyone enjoyed the hot soup – how good it tasted to Jan. The children gathered around the old woman and she told them about the first Christmas in Bethlehem, long ago, and how the Christ child returns each Christmas to see which children love him and welcome him into their homes.

"If I had a home I'd welcome the Christ child," said Jan.

Just then the clock in the town square began to chime midnight.

"It's Christmas Day!" laughed the old woman. "Hurry, let's go to the square and see the people coming out from midnight mass and wish everyone Happy Christmas."

So they did just that, but quite extraordinarily, at the last strike of midnight something wonderful happened. A huge Christmas tree, the biggest and most beautiful ever imagined, suddenly appeared in the square.

"Wow!" said Jan. "Look at that star on the top – it's just like the Bethlehem star."

The star lit up the whole square, the sky, the houses and all the people.

"That tree is just for you Jan," said the child with the lantern. "It's yours! You lovingly gave me the only thing you had in the whole world, your coat."

"But the old woman also gave all she had – she gave me love and soup – so she should share this tree with me," said Jan with a big smile. Someone in the square suddenly recognised the child.

"Look, it's the Christ child!" they shouted.

"Yes," said the Christ child with the lantern. "I could have called you all for help, like Jan did, but you were all too busy. Only Jan and this poor old woman were willing to listen and to share."

With that, the Christ child disappeared. Since that night, the people of Prague have always set up a beautiful Christmas tree in the square and they decorate it with all kinds of gifts for the poor and needy in honour of Jan and the old woman. The people of Prague like to be ready just in case the Christ child should return.

O Little *Town* Of *Bethlehem*

Words by **Phillips Brooks** *Music* **Traditional**

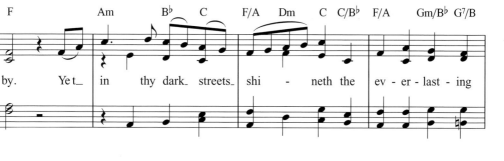

by. Yet in thy dark streets shineth the ev-er-last-ing

light; the hopes and fears of all the years are met in thee to-night.

53

O Little Town Of Bethlehem

2 For Christ is born of Mary;
And, gathered all above,
While mortals sleep, the angels keep
Their watch of wond'ring love.
O morning stars, together
Proclaim the holy birth,
And praises sing to God the King,
And peace to men on earth!

3 How silently, how silently,
The wondrous gift is giv'n!
So God imparts to human hearts
The blessings of his heav'n.
No ear may hear his coming;
But in this world of sin,
Where meek souls will receive him, still
The dear Christ enters in.

4 O holy child of Bethlehem,
Descend to us, we pray;
Cast out our sin, and enter in,
Be born in us today.
We hear the Christmas angels
The great glad tidings tell:
O come to us, abide with us,
Our Lord Emmanuel.

O Little *Town* Of *Bethlehem*

US Tune Words by **Phillips Brooks** *Music by* **Lewis H Redner**

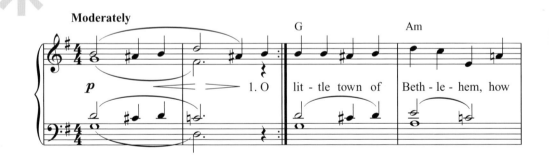

G   G   Am C#dim   B   B⁷   Em B⁷ G   Am   B⁷

by.   Yet   in thy dark streets   shin - eth the   ev - er - last - ing   light;   the

G   Am   C#dim   G   A⁷   D⁷ |1. 2. 3.| ||4.|

                                    G   G

hopes and fears of   all the years are   met in thee   to - night.   2.For   - el.
                                        (see block lyric)

2 For Christ is born of Mary;
And, gathered all above,
While mortals sleep, the angels keep
Their watch of wond'ring love.
O morning stars, together
Proclaim the holy birth,
And praises sing to God the King,
And peace to men on earth!

3 How silently, how silently,
The wondrous gift is giv'n!
So God imparts to human hearts
The blessings of his heav'n.
No ear may hear his coming;
But in this world of sin,
Where meek souls will receive him, still
The dear Christ enters in.

4 O holy child of Bethlehem,
Descend to us, we pray;
Cast out our sin, and enter in,
Be born in us today.
We hear the Christmas angels
The great glad tidings tell:
O come to us, abide with us,
Our Lord Emmanuel.

Once *In* Royal *David's* City

Words by **Cecil Alexander** *Music by* **Henry Gauntlett**

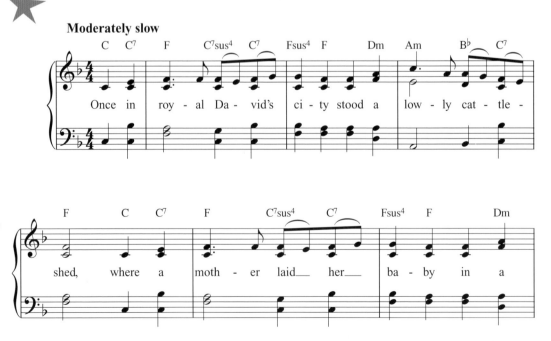

Moderately slow

Once in roy - al Da - vid's ci - ty stood a low - ly cat - tle -

shed, where a moth - er laid her ba - by in a

Children's Christmas Songbook

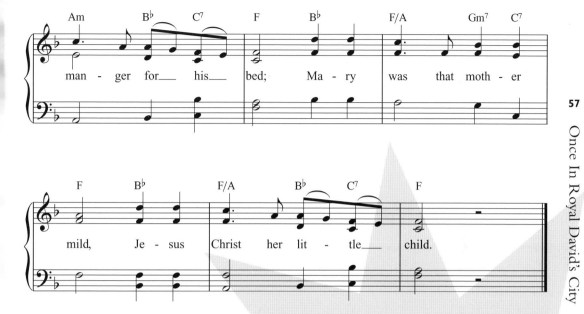

man - ger for_ his_ bed; Ma - ry was that moth - er mild, Je - sus Christ her lit - tle_ child.

2
He came down to earth from heaven,
Who is God and Lord of all,
And his shelter was a stable,
And his cradle was a stall;
With the poor and mean and lowly,
Lived on earth our Saviour holy.

3
And through all his wondrous childhood
He would honour and obey,
Love and watch the lowly maiden,
In whose gentle arms he lay;
Christian children all must be
Mild, obedient, good as He.

4
For He is our childhood's pattern,
Day by day like us he grew,
He was little, weak and helpless,
Tears and smiles like us he knew;
And he feeleth for our sadness,
And he shareth in our gladness.

5
And our eyes at last shall see him
Through his own redeeming love,
For that child so dear and gentle
Is our Lord in heaven above;
And he leads his children on
To the place where he is gone.

6
Not in that poor lowly stable,
With the oxen standing by,
We shall see him; but in heaven,
Set at God's right hand on high;
Where like stars his children crowned
All in white shall wait around.

Past *Three* O'Clock

Words **Traditional** *Music by* **George Woodward**

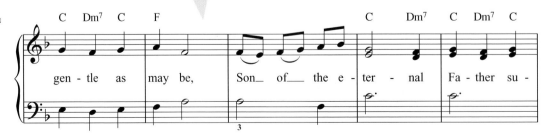

Children's Christmas Songbook

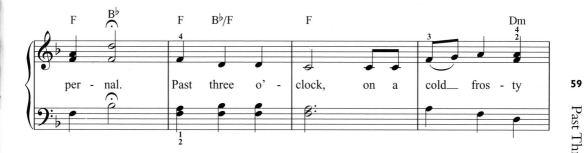

per - nal. Past three o' - clock, on a cold__ fros - ty

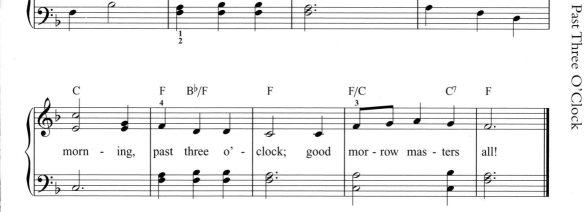

morn - ing, past three o' - clock; good mor - row mas - ters all!

2
Seraph quire singeth,
Angel bell ringeth;
Hark how they rime it,
Time it and chime it.
Past three o'clock…

3
Mid earth rejoices
Hearing such voices
Ne'ertofore so well
Carolling Nowell.
Past three o'clock…

4
Light out of star-land
Leadeth from far land
Princes, to meet him,
Worship and greet him.
Past three o'clock…

5
Myrrh from full coffer,
Incense they offer;
Nor is the golden
Nugget withholden.
Past three o'clock…

6
Thus they: I pray you,
Up, sirs, nor stay you
'Til ye confess him
Likewise, and bless him.
Past three o'clock…

See *Amid* The *Winter's* Snow

Words by **Edward Caswall** *Music by* **John Goss**

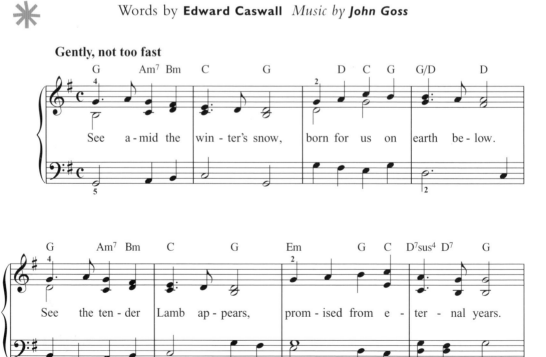

Gently, not too fast

See a-mid the win-ter's snow, born for us on earth be-low.

See the ten-der Lamb ap-pears, prom-ised from e-ter-nal years.

Children's Christmas Songbook

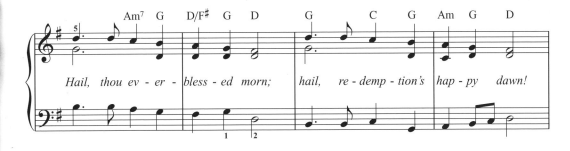

Hail, thou ev - er - bless - ed morn; hail, re - demp - tion's hap - py dawn!

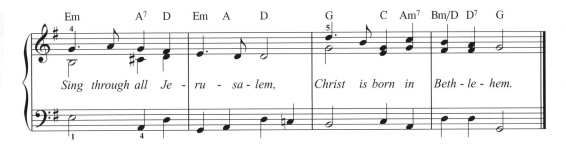

Sing through all Je - ru - sa - lem, Christ is born in Beth - le - hem.

2
Lo, within a manger lies
He who built the starry skies;
He who, throned in heights sublime,
Sits amid the cherubim.
Hail, thou ever-blessed morn…

3
Say, ye holy shepherds, say,
What your joyful news today?
Wherefore have ye left your sheep
On the lonely mountain steep?
Hail, thou ever-blessed morn…

4
'As we watched at dead of night,
Lo, we saw a wondrous light;
Angels, singing peace on earth,
Told us of the Saviour's birth.'
Hail, thou ever-blessed morn…

5
Sacred infant, all divine,
What a tender love was thine,
Thus to come from highest bliss,
Down to such a world as this!
Hail, thou ever-blessed morn…

6
Virgin mother Mary,
By the…

Children's Christmas Songbook

Silent *Night*

Words by **Joseph Mohr** *Music by* **Franz Gruber**

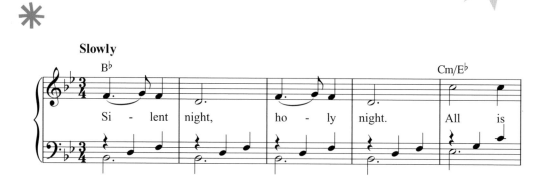

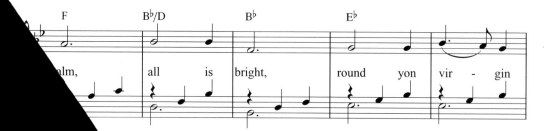

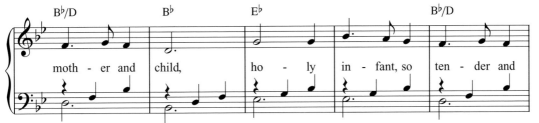

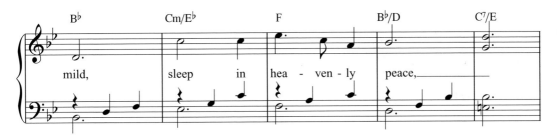

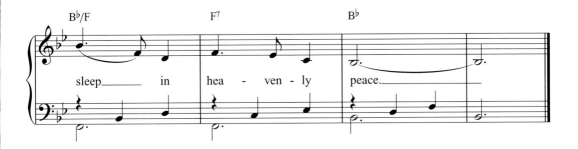

moth - er and child, ho - ly in - fant, so ten - der and

mild, sleep in hea - ven - ly peace,

sleep in hea - ven - ly peace.

2 Silent night, holy night.
Shepherds quake at the sight,
Glories stream from heaven afar,
Heav'nly hosts sing alleluia:
Christ, the Saviour is born,
Christ, the Saviour is born.

3 Silent night, holy night.
Son of God, love's pure light,
Radiant beams from thy holy face,
With the dawn of redeeming grace:
Jesus, Lord, at thy birth,
Jesus, Lord, at thy birth.

The *Holly* And *The* Ivy

Traditional

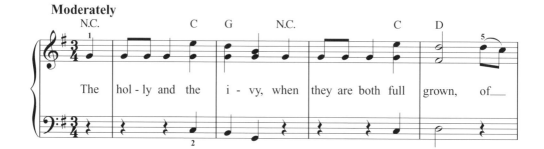

The hol - ly and the i - vy, when they are both full grown, of

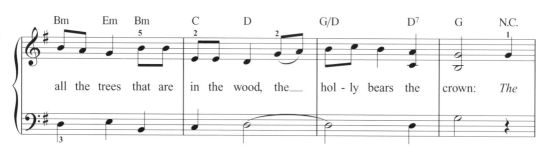

all the trees that are in the wood, the hol - ly bears the crown: *The*

Children's Christmas Songbook

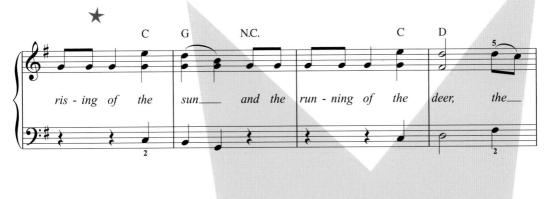

ris - ing of the sun___ and the run - ning of the deer, the___

play - ing of the mer - ry or - gan, sweet sing - ing in the choir.

2 The holly bears a blossom,
White as the lily flow'r,
And Mary bore sweet Jesus Christ
To be our sweet Saviour.
The rising of the sun...

3 The holly bears a berry,
As red as any blood,
And Mary bore sweet Jesus Christ
To do poor sinners good.
The rising of the sun...

4 The holly bears a prickle,
As sharp as any thorn,
And Mary bore sweet Jesus Christ
On Christmas Day in the morn.
The rising of the sun...

5 The holly bears a bark,
As bitter as any gall,
And Mary bore sweet Jesus Christ
For to redeem us all.
The rising of the sun...

6 The holly and the ivy,
When they are both full grown,
Of all the trees that are in the wood,
The holly bears the crown.
The rising of the sun...

We Three Kings Of Orient Are

Words & Music by **John Henry Hopkins**

Smooth and flowing

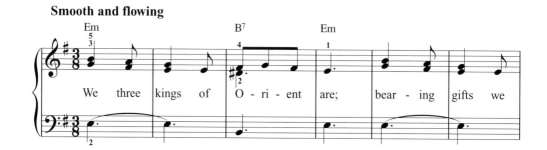

We three kings of O - ri - ent are; bear - ing gifts we

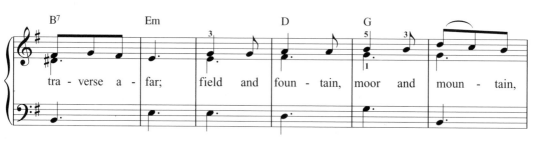

tra - verse a - far; field and foun - tain, moor and moun - tain,

Children's Christmas Songbook

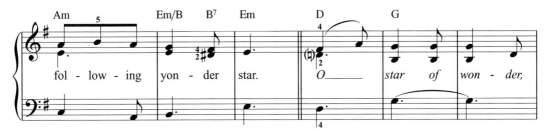

fol - low - ing yon - der star. O_____ star of won - der,

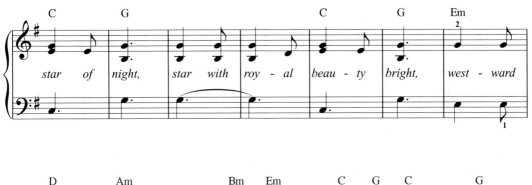

star of night, star with roy - al beau - ty bright, west - ward

lead - ing, still pro - ceed - ing, guide us to thy per - fect light.

2
Born a King on Bethlehem plain,
Gold I bring, to crown him again,
King for ever, ceasing never,
Over us all to reign.
O star of wonder, star of night…

3
Frankincense to offer have I,
Incense owns a Deity nigh,
Prayer and praising, gladly raising,
Worship him, God most high.
O star of wonder, star of night…

4
Myrrh is mine, its bitter perfume
Breathes a life of gathering gloom;
Sorrowing, sighing, bleeding, dying,
Sealed in the stone-cold tomb.
O star of wonder, star of night…

5
Glorious now behold him arise,
King and God and sacrifice;
Alleluia, alleluia,
Earth to heav'n replies.
O star of wonder, star of night…

While *Shepherds* Watched

Words by **Nahum Tate** *Music* **Traditional**

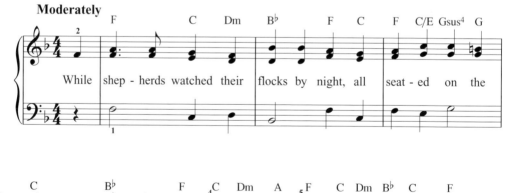

While shep - herds watched their flocks by night, all seat - ed on the ground, the an - gel of the Lord came down, and glo - ry shone a - round.

Children's Christmas Songbook

2 'Fear not,' said he (for mighty dread
Had seized their troubled mind);
'Glad tidings of great joy I bring
To you and all mankind.'

3 'To you in David's town this day
Is born in David's line
A Saviour, who is Christ the Lord;
And this shall be the sign:'

4 'The heav'nly babe you there shall find
To human view displayed,
All meanly wrapped in swathing bands,
And in a manger laid.'

5 Thus spake the seraph, and forthwith
Appeared a shining throng
Of angels praising God, who thus
Addressed their joyful song:

6 'All glory be to God on high,
And to the earth be peace;
Goodwill henceforth from heav'n to men
Begin and never cease.'

Christmas Is Coming

Traditional

Christmas is coming, the geese are getting fat,
Please put a penny in the old man's hat.
If you haven't got a penny, a ha'penny will do.
If you haven't got a ha'penny,
God bless you!

Jingle *Bells*

Words & Music by **J S Pierpont**

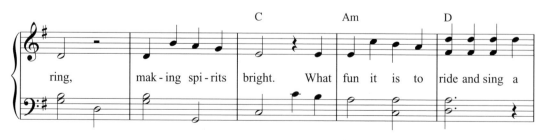

D⁷   G   G   C

sleigh-ing song to - night! *Oh!*   *Jin-gle bells,*   *jin-gle bells,*   *jin-gle all the*

G   Am   D⁷   Gsus⁴ G   A⁷   D

way.   *Oh, what fun it*   *is to ride in a*   *one-horse o-pen*   *sleigh! Oh!*

G   C   G

Jin - gle bells,   *jin - gle bells,*   *jin - gle all the*   *way.*

C   Gsus⁴   G   D⁷   G

Oh, what fun it   *is to ride in a*   *one - horse o-pen*   *sleigh!*

2
Now the ground is white,
Go it while you're young.
Take the girls tonight,
Sing this sleighing song.
Get a bob-tailed bay,
Two-forty for his speed,
Then hitch him to an open sleigh
And crack! You'll take the lead.
Oh! Jingle bells…

Santa's *Party* Jelly

You will need...

Different coloured jellies, including red

Tumblers

Clear honey

White sugar

Ice cream

Make a red jelly according to the maker's instruction,
and allow the liquid to completely cool.
Half fill a small clear glass tumbler with the jelly, and leave it to set
hard in the fridge, propping the glass, so that the jelly sets at an angle.
It is best to get help sorting the fridge out, so that no one
moves your jelly until it is set.

Make a second jelly in a contrasting colour – yellow or pale green.
Wait until the liquid is cold but not set, and add this to the tumbler.
Leave the second jelly to set with the tumbler upright.

Carefully wipe some clear honey around the top rim of the tumbler
and sprinkle sugar onto the honey, so that it looks like frosting.
Before serving Santa's party jelly, spoon some ice cream on the top.

Rudolph's *Dinner*

You will need...

Bread

Butter

Mincemeat

Apple or Orange juice

Shredded Wheat

Ice cream

Cut narrow strips of buttered bread and spread thickly with
mincemeat moistened with a little apple or orange juice.
Place the strips on a baking tray and put in the oven for about
5 minutes until the bread is toasted.

Separate a Shredded Wheat biscuit (Rudolph's hay) onto a
flat plate and serve the mincemeat slices on top.
Be careful, as mincemeat gets very hot in the oven.
When cool, add a scoop of soft ice cream.

Star *Biscuits*

You will need...

2oz (55g) icing sugar

6oz (175g) of plain flour

4oz (115g) of butter

1 tablespoon of milk

Half a teaspoon of vanilla essence

Star shaped biscuit cutter (optional)

Boiled sweets

Combine the icing sugar, plain flour, butter, milk
and vanilla essence in a large bowl.

Mix everything together with finger tips, breaking up the lumps,
until the mixture becomes a pliable dough.
Keep working it, and it will eventually turn into a dough.
Cover with cling film and put in the fridge for 45 minutes.

Roll out the dough on a lightly floured board until it is
about half a centimetre thick. Cut out star shapes – if you have
a cutter this may be easier but perhaps not such fun!

Using a skewer, make one small hole in a tip of the star, but not too close to the edge. Put the star biscuits on non stick baking paper. Push a small boiled sweet down into the centre of each biscuit making sure the sweet gets right through to the baking paper. Bake for 7 minutes in an oven set to gas mark 6 (400° F).

The sweets will have melted and the biscuits cooked to a light brown. Leave the biscuits until they are completely cool, then thread ribbon or pretty parcel string through the little hole. Hang the biscuits on the tree or keep in an airtight tin.

Christmas *Shapes*

Using the same recipe as *Star Biscuits*, roll out the dough and cut out shapes with Christmas biscuit cutters, placing them on cooking parchment on a baking tray. Pop them in an oven set to gas mark 6 (400° F), and check if the biscuits are golden after six minutes.

When they are cooked, leave them to cool, then decorate them as you wish with ready made icing tubes available from most supermarkets.

Jack Frost
Alison Hedger

Jack Frost comes and Jack Frost goes,
He numbs my nose and tickles my toes.
Jack Frost comes and Jack Frost goes.

Marzipan *Mice*

You will need...

Marzipan

Raisins

Take one piece of ready made marzipan and form into a mouse's body shape.
Elongate the mouse's head to have a pointed nose.
Pinch up two ears. Make a tail by cutting a length of string and pushing
it into the body with a skewer. Make more mice varying in size to
make a family of adults and young ones. Eyes can be made with the skewer,
or with two little bits of raisin. Leave the mice to dry out.

A *Winter* Warmer

You will need...

Blackcurrant juice

Apple juice

Runny honey

Lemon juice

Slices of orange and lemon

Combine some blackcurrant and apple juice with some hot water.
(Be careful not to use boiling water – only very warm.) Stir in a spoonful or
two of runny honey and a squeeze of lemon juice.
Decorate the tumbler with slices of orange and lemon, as if a cocktail.

Peppermint
Christmas Sweeties

You will need...

9oz (250g) icing sugar

Half an egg white

1 teaspoon of peppermint flavour

2 teaspoons of lemon juice

Desiccated/dried coconut

Different coloured food dyes

Cutters in different shapes

Rolling pin

Baking sheet covered in cling film

Sift the icing sugar into a large bowl, taking care not to spill the powdered sugar around too much! Mix the egg white, a few drops of peppermint flavouring and the lemon juice in a cup.
Add this mixture little by little to the icing sugar, until the mixture binds together, it may be rather sticky.

Form the mixture into interesting shapes like worms and blobs.
You can also use different shaped cutters if you wish.
Roll your peppermint worms in desiccated coconut for a spiky effect.
Dip the blobs into melted chocolate, and also decorate them with red and green glace cherries. Leave your sweets to set hard for about an hour.
These peppermint sweeties are great as gifts! Place them on tissue paper in a pretty box, tie with a festive ribbon and give to friends and family.

Christmas *Pops*

You will need...

3oz (85g) of Rice Crispies

3oz (85g) of desiccated/dried coconut

3oz (85g) icing sugar

3oz (85g) full cream milk powder

3oz (85g) mixed dried fruit

3oz (85g) glace cherries

8oz (225g) butter

Mix the Rice Crispies, desiccated coconut, icing sugar,
full cream milk powder, mixed dried fruit and
glace cherries in a large bowl.
Gently melt the butter in a pan. Don't let the melted butter get hot,
it must just be warm. Add the melted butter to the dried
ingredients and stir well.

Press the mixture into a tin lined with non stick baking paper and
chill overnight in the fridge. Cut into little pieces and put each piece into
a mini paper cake case. Arrange your Christmas pops on a serving dish
garnished with a piece of holly.

Yule *Log*

You will need...

Plain chocolate swiss roll

Chocolate icing

White icing sugar

Spread chocolate icing over a plain chocolate swiss roll. Drag a fork
lengthwise down the cake to give the icing a rough texture, like tree bark.
Decorate the log with a bow, or a plastic robin or holly.
Sprinkle some icing sugar over the log to look like snow.

Christmas *Milkshake*

You will need (*per person*)...

Cup of cold milk

Scoop of vanilla ice cream

A few small ice cubes

Half a banana

A tiny bit of cinnamon

Green and red glace cherries

Blend everything together until smooth, and pour into a clear tumbler.
Sprinkle icing sugar on the top and float one green and one red glace cherry
in the milkshake to add some Christmas colour.

Santa's *Sack*

Play this in an area cleared of furniture.
Fill a large plastic bin bag with things that will make a clanging noise when they bang against each other; perhaps some empty drink cans and stones.
(Don't use anything that will break!)
Everyone is blindfolded except Santa who carries the sack.
Santa noisily shakes the sack and everyone tries to grab it by listening out for where it is.
The first person to grab the sack takes over as Santa.

Card *Jigsaws* Hide & Seek

This game is fun to play with several people. Make sure each player
has an *old* Christmas card. Before you start playing, cut the front
pictures of each card into 6 shapes which when reassembled make a jigsaw.
Keep just one piece of each picture and hide the other
pieces around the room or about the house. Give each player the
first piece of their jigsaw and then ask them to find the rest of their picture.
The winner is the first person to complete their jigsaw.

Drawing *People*

Each person has a plain strip of paper about 29cm x 10cm.
Each person secretly draws a hat (any shape and design) and then folds
the paper over towards themselves to conceal their drawing.
The pieces of paper are then passed around to the next person.
Everyone now draws a face below the concealed hat. Again fold over
the paper and pass it to the next person, and continue to draw at subsequent
turns an upper body and arms, waist to above the knees
and knees to feet. Finally add a name and pass on for the last time.
Now each person unravels the piece of paper they are holding to
reveal a very funny person!

Draw in the following order…
1. Hat
2. Face
3. Neck to waist, including arms
4. Waist to above knees
5. Knees to feet
6. The character name
7. Unfolding the picture

Story Consequences

This is much like the drawing people game,
except words are used, not drawings.
Each person has a plain strip of paper and writes as follows,
concealing their writing and passing the paper on.

1. Male character name ....
2. Met .... (a female character name)
3. At ....
4. He said to her ....
5. She said to him ....
6. The consequence was ....
7. Each short story is read out by the person holding the piece of paper after the last pass.

Finger *Footie*

Cut a snowman and a Christmas tree shape from a cereal box.
Cut two finger holes in each shape, as shown and then paint the shapes.
When dry, put two fingers through the holes and flick a
cotton wool football with the fingers. Have two goal lines, the snowman
playing against the Christmas tree. The idea is to score goals –
whoever scores the most in a set time wins!

Baboushka

Traditional Russian tale retold by Alison Hedger

Baboushka was always sweeping and dusting – she liked everything to be 'just so'! One dark winter's day there was a loud knock at her front door. Three very important looking men stood there, asking if she knew where they could find the baby Christ King.

"Gracious me, no," said Baboushka. "Why should I know? But please come in anyway." The three men sat down in Baboushka's kitchen and enjoyed a drink and a piece of homemade bread.

"Thank you most kindly," said the men as they prepared to leave. "We can't stop for long as we must find the baby Christ King and give him our presents of gold, frankincense and myrrh." With that they left, calling out as they went, "Why don't you come with us?"

"I can't," said Baboushka, "I must sweep up all the crumbs and wash the cups." Baboushka watched the three men disappear over the hill.

"I really would have liked to have gone with them and found the baby Christ King," she said out loud. "I know! I'll set off at first light in the morning, and go in the same direction as the three men. I expect it will be easy enough to find the child."

That evening Baboushka emptied an old toy chest and dusted all the little wooden toys that had belonged to her grown up children. She carefully put them into a basket. Next morning as the sun was just about to peek over the horizon, Baboushka set off with her basket, to follow the three important men, but she walked for miles and miles, never meeting anyone who had seen the men, and no one had heard of the baby Christ King. So just to be sure that she didn't pass by the baby King unknowingly, Baboushka placed a toy on each door step as she went along – just in case!

That's why in Russia on the twelfth night of Christmas, children find a special little something left for them from Baboushka.

Children's Christmas Songbook

Robin *Redbreast*

Traditional North Canadian story retold by Alison Hedger

Long ago and far away in the icy Arctic wastes, a hungry polar bear watched as a man and his small son made a fire inside their igloo. They needed to keep themselves warm during the long, bitter night. The bear thought:

"If I put that fire out, the man and his son will freeze to death overnight. Then I can have their frozen bodies to eat in the morning."

So when the two were asleep, the polar bear put his paw into the igloo and patted out the fire. Off he went, thinking how clever he was! Unknown to the bear, a little brown bird had been watching. While the bear's back was turned, she hopped into the igloo. It was so cold without the fire that the breath from the sleeping man and boy was freezing around their noses! The bird flapped her wings at the last ember in the fire. She flapped and flapped, until the fire was at last rekindled. A few flaps later and the fire roared back into life! As she did this, her breast turned red with the heat and THAT is why Robins have a red breast.

The Snow Lies White
Traditional

The snow lies white on roof and tree,
Frost fairies creep about,
The world's as still as it can be,
And Santa Claus is out.

He's making haste his gifts to leave,
While the stars show his way,
There'll soon be no more Christmas Eve,
Tomorrow's Christmas Day!

Festive *Napkin* Rings

You will need...

An old Sellotape ring, big enough for a napkin

Festive ribbon

Different coloured felt

Napkin

Find some used Sellotape rings and wrap Christmas patterned ribbon around them. Then cut out different festive items using felt. You could have sprigs of holly, a Christmas tree, a Christmas pudding or a snowman! Once you have made your Christmas item, stick it to the napkin ring and wait to dry.

MOST CRAFTS ON PAGES 86-94 WILL REQUIRE SCISSORS, GLUE OR STICKY TAPE, AND A RULER

ALWAYS MAKE SURE AN ADULT IS SUPERVISING WHEN USING SCISSORS

Angels *In A Row*

You will need...

A piece of A4 paper

Coloured pens and other decorative materials

Glitter Glue (optional)

Fold a piece of A4 paper in half and in the same direction, fold it in half again (this will give you four angels in a row). Trace around the template on this page – you can use grease-proof or thin paper to do this. Cut it out and draw around it onto the top outside of the folded paper, making sure the wings go right up to the edges of the paper.

Cut out the shape going through all the layers of paper.
Unfold the angels and draw faces and colour in as you like.
Some edging in pretty glitter glue would look good.

Alternatively make angels from folded newspaper or large pieces of used wrapping paper. The cut-outs look especially lovely if made in gold and silver paper.

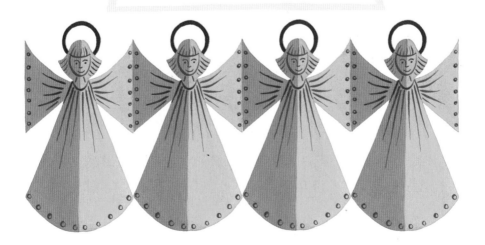

Christmas *Sweetie* Horn

You will need...

Coloured thin card

Decorative bits and pieces

Ribbon

Cut a piece of coloured thin card into a square about 15cm x 15cm
and roll into a cone shape, overlapping the join. Fix the join with sticky tape,
and decorate the horn with bits of tinsel, holly or stars.
Make a hole in the top edge of the horn and thread some parcel ribbon
through the hole to make a loop.
Fill the horn with sweets and hang it on the Christmas tree.

Christmas *Mobile*

You will need...

Metal coat hanger

Ribbon

Tinsel

Old Christmas cards

Cotton thread

Bind ribbon around a metal coat hanger and finish off with a bow below
the hook, or wrap tinsel around the hanger, fixing with sticky tape.
Cut characters and scenes from the Christmas story from old Christmas cards,
and attach each one to the cross piece of the hanger with cotton thread.
Make sure the weight of the mobile pictures is evenly distributed,
and that each picture is on different length threads.
Vary the cut-out designs, using circles, triangles, squares and stars.

Fairy *Finger* Puppets

CUT OUT

DRAW

You will need...

Thin white card

Coloured pens

Decorative materials

GLUE

Trace the fairy shape on this page and cut out. You can use grease-proof or thin paper to do this. Now draw around it onto a piece of card TWICE. Cut out the shapes and colour in and decorate ONE of them to make it look like a pretty fairy.

Now carefully put some glue - not too much – around the outer edges of the other fairy shape and stick the decorated one on top of the one with glue. Wait to dry and place on finger! Do this once more and you can perform the poem *Two Little Fairies* on page 96.

No *Glue*
Rudolph's *Hoof*
Paper *Chains*

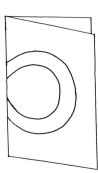

You will need...

Link template

Used cereal box

Paper

Coloured pens

Trace the link on this page, shaped like Rudolph's hoof-print and cut out.
Draw around it onto some card from an old cereal box and cut out.
This your link template. Fold your paper in half and lay the template onto
one side as shown above and draw around it, making sure the
straight end of the hoof is on the fold.

Cut out the hoof taking care not to cut through the folds.
Colour and decorate the links if using plain paper. These chains will look great
if made from different coloured paper. Connect the links as shown.

Scrunchy *Snowman*

You will need...

Used cereal box

White and coloured tissue paper

Brightly coloured card

Coloured paper or cloth (optional)

Cut out a snowman shape from a cereal box. Scrunch white tissue paper
into small balls and glue them inside the snowman shape.
Add eyes, nose, mouth, buttons and a hat – these can be scrunched coloured
tissue paper, or flat pieces of coloured paper or cloth stuck onto the snowman.
To display your snowman, stick him onto a piece of brightly coloured card.

Why not try making a scrunchy Christmas tree or
scrunchy Christmas pudding?

Upright *Christmas* Tree

You will need...

Stiff paper

Coloured tissue paper (including green and brown)

Pencil

1. Cut a large semicircle from a piece of stiff paper, marking a 'don't stick' border along half of the straight edge.
2. Cut plenty of 3cm x 3cm squares of green tissue paper.
3. One by one, place each tissue square over the non-writing end of a pencil, gently flattening the tissue paper edges down around the pencil end. Hold the paper with thumb and forefinger.
4. Dip the tissue, still held on the pencil end, into glue and then place it onto the cut out stiff paper semicircle (not on the 'don't stick' border).
5. Gently pull the pencil away leaving the green tissue stuck in place.
6. Repeat this until the semicircle is covered with green tissue and leave to dry.
7. Fold the semicircle into a cone shape with the 'don't stick' border slipping inside the cone. Stick this in place with tape.
8. Your Christmas tree can be decorated further if you wish.

Perhaps you may like to have some of the green tissue replaced with red, blue or yellow tissue, which will give the effect of the tree being decorated with fairy lights. The tree done this way will look very real.

POINT OF TREE

DO NOT STICK

Window *Cards*

You will need...

Card

Coloured pens and other decorative materials

Fold a piece of card in half and mark out the shape of a window on the front. Carefully cut away the window panes so that you can see through the front to the inside. Decorate your card as you wish, remembering to have something showing through each window pane when the card is shut. Younger children will find arched windows easier to draw, cut out and design.

Paper *Plate* Portraits

You will need...

Thin coloured card

Paper plate

Photograph or picture

Cut out lots of green holly leaves and yellow stars from thin card. Stick the shapes around the rim of a paper plate. Now fill in the centre of the plate with a portrait. This is best done on plain white paper, then trimmed and stuck in place, or could be a photograph.

A Visit From St Nicholas

Clement Clark Moore

'Twas the night before Christmas, when all through the house
Not a creature was stirring, not even a mouse;
The stockings were hung by the chimney with care,
In hopes that St Nicholas soon would be there;
The children were nestled all snug in their beds,
While visions of sugar-plums danced in their heads;
And mamma in her 'kerchief, and I in my cap,
Had just settled down for a long winter's nap,
When out on the lawn there arose such a clatter,
I sprang from the bed to see what was the matter.
Away to the window I flew like a flash,
Tore open the shutters and threw up the sash.
The moon on the breast of the new-fallen snow
Gave the lustre of mid-day to objects below,
When, what to my wondering eyes should appear,
But a miniature sleigh, and eight tiny reindeer,
With a little old driver, so lively and quick,
I knew in a moment it must be St Nick.
More rapid than eagles his coursers they came,
And he whistled, and shouted, and called them by name;
"Now, Dasher! now, Dancer! now, Prancer and Vixen!
On, Comet! on Cupid! on, Donner and Blitzen!
To the top of the porch, to the top of the wall,
Now dash away! dash away! dash away all!"
As dry leaves that before the wild hurricane fly,
When they meet with an obstacle, mount to the sky,
So up to the house-top the coursers they flew,
With the sleigh full of toys, and St Nicholas too.
And then, in a twinkling, I heard on the roof
The prancing and pawing of each little hoof.
As I drew in my head, and was turning around,
Down the chimney St Nicholas came with a bound.
He was dressed all in fur, from his head to his foot,
And his clothes were all tarnished with ashes and soot;
A bundle of toys he had flung on his back,
And he looked like a pedlar just opening his pack.
His eyes - how they twinkled! His dimples - how merry!
His cheeks were like roses, his nose like a cherry.
His droll little mouth was drawn up like a bow,
And the beard of his chin was as white as the snow;
The stump of a pipe he held tight in his teeth,
And the smoke it encircled his head like a wreath;
He had a broad face and a little round belly,
That shook, when he laughed like a bowlful of jelly.
He was chubby and plump, a right jolly old elf,
And I laughed when I saw him, in spite of myself;
A wink of his eye and a twist of his head,
Soon gave me to know I had nothing to dread.
He spoke not a word, but went straight to his work,
And filled all the stockings; then turned with a jerk,
And laying his finger aside of his nose,
And giving a nod, up the chimney he rose;
He sprang to his sleigh, to his team gave a whistle,
And away they all flew like the down of a thistle.
But I heard him exclaim, 'ere he drove out of sight,
"Happy Christmas to all, and to all a good-night."

A C T I O N
R H Y M E S

Two Little Fairies

A small piece of wet tissue paper is stuck to the nails of each
index finger – these are Klara and Kitty. Alternatively, you can make your
own fairy finger puppets (see page 90).

During 'Fly away...' each hand is raised to behind the ears and when
the hands are brought down, the index fingers have been tucked away and
the middle fingers are shown. The hands are raised again to the ears on
'Come back...' and the middle fingers without the tissue paper are changed for
the index fingers, so bringing back the two fairies!

This is a traditional game rhyme, better known as
Two Little Dickie Birds Sitting On A Wall.

Two Little Fairies
Adapted by Alison Hedger

Two little fairies looking very pretty:
One called Klara, one called Kitty.
Fly away Klara, fly away Kitty.
Come back Klara, come back Kitty.

Christmas Robin
Alison Hedger

Christmas robin hop-hop-hop,
Hopping, hopping never stopping.
Christmas robin look and see,
Here's a wriggly worm for tea!

Little Snowdrop
Alison Hedger

Little snowdrop white not red,
Won't you nod your pretty head?
Nid-nod, niddy-nod, nid-nid-nod!